8/95

J
793.8
DAY   Day, Jon

Magic

MAGIC

JON DAY

With photographs by Zul Mukhida

Thomson Learning • New York

First published in the
United States in 1995 by
Thomson Learning
115 Fifth Avenue
New York, NY 10003

First published in Great Britain in 1994 by
Wayland (Publishers) Ltd.

Library of Congress Cataloging-in-Publication Data
Day, Jon.
Magic / Jon Day ; with photographs by Zul Mukhida.
     p.   cm.
Includes bibliographical references and index.
ISBN 1-56847-198-X
1. Tricks—Juvenile literature. [1. Magic tricks.]
I. Mukhida, Zul, ill. II. Title.
GV1548.D295   1994
793.8—dc20   94-18141

Printed in Italy

CONTENTS

AN INTRODUCTION TO MAGIC

We all know that there is no such thing as real magic. When you see a magician working at a birthday party or on television, you see someone who is using his or her hands and head, very cleverly, to fool you. This is not meant to make you look foolish – just to fool you into thinking that something has happened that has probably not happened at all. In other words, the magician tricks you!

I will show you how to trick people (in a harmless way, of course) so that you will be able to amuse and entertain your friends. I will also explain to you a little about the fascinating history of this wonderful pastime.

So jump onto my magic carpet! Hold on to your hat! You are about the enter the "Amazing World of Magic!"

HOW TO BECOME A MAGICIAN

In order to become a good magician, you need to concentrate on two things. The first is **practice**. Practice each trick over and over again until you can almost do it with your eyes shut. Only then will you be ready to show the trick to your friends. Practice in front of a mirror so that you can see what other people will see.

The second thing you must learn is **presentation**. If you just go through the stages of a trick, in a mechanical way, your audience will find it very boring. Presentation means dressing up the trick, with extra actions and words, so that it becomes magical, not just mechanical.

There are several things you can do to improve your presentation. Try writing out what you plan to say. The words are as important as the trick itself.

You could use a tape recorder to record the words and keep playing them back until you have memorized them.

You could dress up like a magician, with a cape and a hat. A magic wand is also a useful thing to have. Make one out of a dowel rod (you can buy one from a hardware store). Paint it black in the middle and white at each end, using water-based paints such as poster paints or powder paints. To make the wand glossy, coat it with clear varnish. If you cannot make a wand, an unsharpened pencil will do.

Remember that a magician is really an actor pretending to be a magician. But your audience must believe that *you* think you are performing real magic. If *you* don't seem to believe it, you can't expect other people to believe it.

THREE GOLDEN RULES

1 Check that you have everything prepared *before* you start doing the trick. This means having *everything* ready and in the right place.

2 Never do the same trick twice. You may be asked to do it again. This means that your trick has been successful and your audience wants another chance to figure it out – so don't fall for it!

3 Keep your secrets. If everyone knows how your tricks are done, there is really no point in doing them anymore. You can, of course, share your secrets with fellow magicians – but nobody else.

EGYPT: THE CUPS AND BALLS

Our magic carpet takes us first to Egypt. The year is 2500 B.C.
The first ever known magician, Teta (sometimes translated as Dedi), lived in Egypt at this time. It is said that Teta could eat 500 loaves of bread and a shoulder of beef and drink 100 jugs of beer, every day. He was very fat – and no wonder!
This is a version of one of his less fattening tricks!

What happens

Paper balls seem to pass through the bottoms of solid cups and appear beneath them. Then one of the balls disappears, and is found under another cup three feet away.

What you need

Three paper cups
Four tissue paper balls about 2 inches across. Make them all the same size and color.
A magic wand

Preparation

The audience only sees three balls. No one ever knows about the fourth one. That is the secret! Stack the cups with one ball hidden inside the middle cup. Lay out the other three balls in a row.

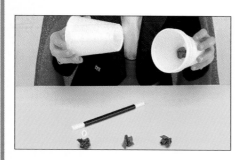

What you do

1 Pick up all three cups in one hand. Pull off the bottom cup with your other hand.

2 Turn it over very quickly and place it, mouth down, on the table.

Do the same with the next cup. Do this smoothly, and with the cup mouth turned slightly toward you. In this way, the hidden ball will not fall out or be seen.

3 Place the third cup down in the same way. Now put a paper ball on top of the middle cup. This is the one with the hidden ball beneath it.

4 Stack the other two cups on top of the middle cup and ball. Tap the stack with the magic wand.

5 Lift up all three cups together to show that the ball has magically fallen through! You still have a ball *secretly* hidden in the middle cup.

6 Lay the three cups out again as before, but this time place the middle cup over the ball that has just "appeared."

Place a ball on top of it, cover with the other two cups, tap with the wand, then lift the cups to show that there are now *two* balls under the cups.

7 Do it all again – this time placing the middle cup over the two balls. Tap with the wand and lift up the stack to show *three* balls.

8 Now pull off the bottom cup and place it down to your left. Pull off the next cup and place it down to your right.

Put a ball on top of the left cup and cover it with the third cup. Tap with the wand.

9 Lift up the two cups to your left. Look amazed that the ball is not underneath them. Turn to look at the right cup. Tap it with the wand. Lift it up and show that the ball has somehow "jumped across!"

7

GREECE: THE GREEK MARBLES

Our magic carpet now takes us to ancient Greece. The ancient Greeks built wonderful houses out of a hard, shiny stone called marble. A famous Greek magician was a beautiful woman named Circe. She could turn people into pigs – or so the story goes! She lived on an island in a marble palace. For this trick, find four small, glass marbles that look alike. You will also need a coin.

What happens

You appear to put just two marbles into your hand, but when you open your fist you are holding three marbles! Then, you put three marbles into your hand. You pull them out one at a time. But when you open your fist, you are also holding a coin that has magically appeared!

Preparation

Note: If you are left-handed, read *left* for *right* and *right* for *left* throughout.
Put the coin in your right pocket. Lay out three marbles on the table. Hold the fourth marble hidden in your right hand.

What you do

1 Hold your left hand out, palm up. Pick up a marble with your right hand and place it on your left palm. (You are still secretly holding another marble.)

2 Pick up another marble and place it on your left hand with the other one. *At the same time,* drop in the hidden marble, too, and close your left hand into a fist. Your audience will think you are holding two marbles when in fact you are holding three.

3 Your right hand is now empty. Openly pick up the last marble from the table and put your hand in your pocket with it.

Then bring out your right hand, with the marble once again hidden in it.

4 Ask: " How many marbles have I got in my hand?"

Answer: "Two."

6 Show that there are three marbles in your left hand again. Place them in a line on the table. Pick them up, one at a time, and place them into your left hand. As you drop in the third marble, secretly drop the coin in too, and close your hand into a fist.

7 With the finger and thumb of your right hand, reach into your left fist. Remove the marbles, one at a time, and put them into your pocket. Count them out loud as you do so. Say, "One, two, three."

8 Keep your left fist closed. Ask: "If I have put three marbles into my pocket, how many marbles are left in my hand?" You will get all sorts of answers. Prove them all wrong by slowly opening your left hand to show that you are holding a shiny coin instead.

Open your hand to show that you have *three* marbles.

5 Now do steps 1 and 2 again. When you reach step 3, put your hand into your pocket with the marble as before. But, this time, leave the marble in your pocket and bring out the coin instead (hidden in your hand).

ITALY: THE QUICK ITALIAN COIN TRICK

The next stop on our magic carpet ride is Rome, the capital of Italy.
In ancient times, over 2,000 years ago, Roman armies conquered much of
Europe. The Romans ruled many countries and introduced great new ideas, such
as building straight roads between towns and cities and warming houses with
central heating. Roman pottery and coins are still dug up all over Europe today.
This trick is another marvel from ancient Italy.

What happens

A small coin is dropped
down your sleeve and
magically plucked through
the cloth at your elbow!

What you need

Just one small coin. (You can
borrow it from your
audience.)

Preparation

First, learn this simple way to
make a coin "vanish."

1 Hold the coin between
your forefinger and thumb.

2 Force your finger and
thumb together with a *snap*.
The coin seems to vanish.

In fact, the coin is lying flat
and is hidden from view by
the flesh of your finger and
thumb.

What you do

1 If you are right-handed, sit with your left arm bent. Rest your elbow on a table, if you prefer. If you are left-handed, bend your right arm.

2 "Snap vanish" the coin directly over your sleeve opening. It will look like you have dropped the coin down your sleeve.

3 Now pluck at the cloth at your elbow a few times. Then magically produce the coin again!

GREAT BRITAIN: A ONE-WAY STREET

As our magic carpet touches down in Great Britain, we find a land steeped in magical history. The famous Merlin was magician to the court of King Arthur in the sixth century A.D. – but nobody knows if he really existed.

However, here are some magic facts about Great Britain that we know for certain:

- The first British magician we know about was a man named Brandon, who performed at the court of King Henry VIII in 1520.

- In 1814, John Henry Anderson was born. He became known as "The Great Wizard of the North." He was the first magician to produce a rabbit out of a hat!

- In 1100, a deck of playing cards was brought to Great Britain from abroad for the very first time.

- In 1571, a man was put in jail for performing card tricks. He was charged with witchcraft.

Try the card trick described here – "A One-Way Street." Don't worry – you won't be charged with witchcraft!

What happens

A friend or a member of your audience chooses a card from a deck of playing cards and replaces it. You find it again, even though the person thoroughly shuffles the cards and you do not look at them.

What you need

A deck of playing cards with a *picture*, not a pattern, on the backs of the cards.

Preparation

Sort out the deck of cards so that all the back designs are facing the same way.

What you do

1 Carefully spread the deck of cards out in a line across a table.

2 Ask someone (let's call the person Sarah) to remove any card from the deck. Tell her to look at it and remember it. In case she forgets, tell her to show it to someone else. Warn them not to whisper what it is. Let's say it is the two of hearts.

3 While she is doing this, sweep up the rest of the cards, from left to right, using your left hand.

4 Place the deck in your right hand. As you do so, twist the deck around so that the pictures on the backs of the cards are now upside down.

5 Ask Sarah to replace her card anywhere in the deck. As long as she has not turned her card upside down too, hers will now be the only one with its picture the opposite way from the rest. If she *has* turned her card around, quickly turn the deck around once more before she returns her card. Just pass the deck from one hand to the other, turning the deck as you do so. This makes it look less obvious.

6 Ask Sarah to shuffle the deck of cards. Take the deck back. Spread the cards between your hands, looking for the edge of Sarah's card. It should stick out like a sore thumb!

7 When you see the card, just cut the deck to bring Sarah's card to the top and place the deck down on the table. (Tap it with a magic wand if you like.)

8 Ask Sarah to name her card.

She will answer: "It was the two of hearts."

You say: "Please turn over the top card, Sarah."

Watch her face when she realizes that it is her card.

UNITED STATES: THE GREAT ESCAPE

We leave Europe and fly across the Atlantic Ocean to the United States. The first known American magician was Jacob Meyer, born in 1735 in Philadelphia. Taking the name of his home city, he called himself Jacob Philadelphia. Strangely enough, he never performed in his own country. The most famous American magician, however, was the Hungarian-born Harry Houdini. Houdini, whose name was Ehrich Weiss until he changed it to honor Jean-Eugène Robert-Houdin, performed in the early 1900s. He was an escapologist. He could escape from anything, anywhere. No prison cell, no chains, no handcuffs could hold him.

This is a trick in honor of Harry Houdini.

What happens

A ring is tied on to a piece of string. Both ends of the string are held by a member of the audience. A handkerchief is thrown over both the ring and the string. You reach underneath and instantly bring out the ring. It has "escaped" from the string!

What you need

A piece of string, about 3 feet long
A clean handkerchief
A finger ring (you can borrow one from a member of your audience)

What you do

The secret of this trick is a special, false knot. You can tie it in front of your audience – but be careful not to let anyone watch too closely.

1 Fold the string in half and push the loop through the ring.

2 Then pull the loop back and over the ring.

3 Now pull both ends of the string tightly.

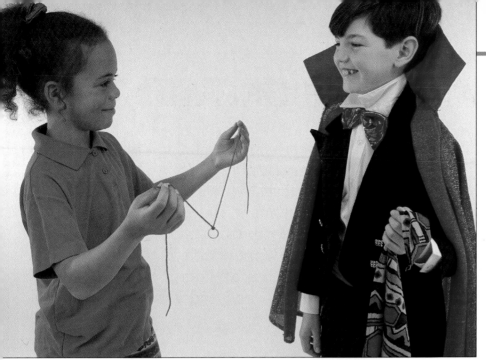

1 Ask someone (let's call her Marie) to hold both ends of the string.

2 Drape the handkerchief over the ring. Now place both your hands beneath the handkerchief. Ask Marie to bring her hands a little closer together (to give a little slack in the string).

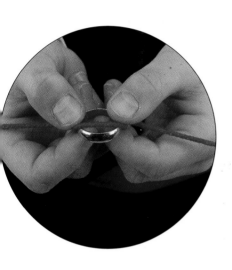

3 To remove the ring, just push the loop of string back up and over it. This action is hidden by the handkerchief and is possible because of the slack in the string.

4 Bring the ring out with a flourish and whip the handkerchief off at the same time. The person is left holding the string. Even the "knot" has vanished!

15

INDIA: THE RIBBON TRICK

Now we fly to India. This is a land where magic has been a part of everyday life for centuries.
One Indian trick in particular has amused and puzzled travelers from other parts of the world more than any other. It is the famous "Indian Rope Trick."
It is always performed outdoors. The magician throws the end of a long rope up into the air. It stays there! Then a little boy climbs up to the top of the rope and…disappears.

Here is a rope trick for you to try – or rather a ribbon trick.

What happens

A piece of ribbon is snipped in two, and then is magically put back together again.

What you need

A piece of ribbon, about 3 feet long
A pair of scissors
An envelope

Preparation

1 Seal the envelope. Then cut off a thin strip from each end. Open the envelope so that you have a paper tube.

2 Make a secret cut, about 2 inches long, across the envelope at the center. Only cut through one layer of paper – do *not* cut all the way through the envelope.

Place the paper tube, ribbon, and scissors on a table before you start.

What you do

1 Pick up the paper tube. Look through it at the audience to show that it is empty. Make sure your fingers cover the secret slit.

4 Pick up the scissors and start to cut the paper tube in half, upward, across the center till you reach the slit. Push the point of the scissors *underneath* the ribbon.

5 Then continue to cut the tube until it is in two pieces. Do not separate them – just hold everything together.

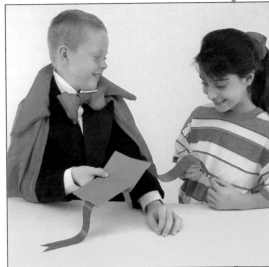

2 Hold the tube by one edge in your left hand (or right hand if you are left-handed). Pass one end of the ribbon through the tube.

3 If you bend the tube a little, you will be able to see the ribbon through your secret slit.

Now hold everything in your left hand (or right hand if you are left-handed).

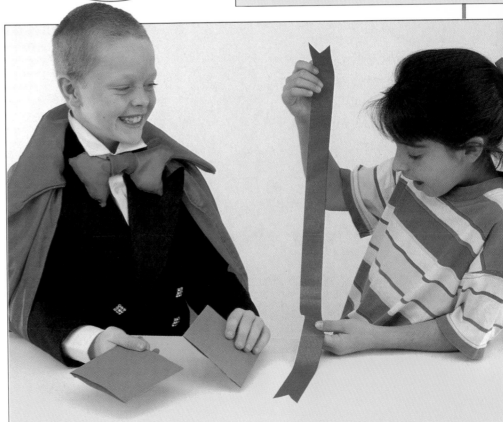

6 Say the magic word: "Abracadabra." Then ask someone to pull one end of the ribbon. It is all in one piece!

CHINA: THE CHINESE HOOPS

Now we fly even farther east, and our magic carpet lands in the country of China. The Chinese have invented many useful things, including paper, stirrups, and gunpowder. In the tenth century, they produced the very first deck of playing cards. If you ever get the chance to watch a Chinese magician, you are in for a real treat.

Here is a Chinese paper trick that you will have lots of fun with.

What happens

You give two people a large paper hoop and a pair of scissors each. You have a paper hoop and scissors, too. All the hoops look identical.

Each person cuts all the way around the center of his or her hoop. You end up with two separate hoops. One person ends up with two hoops that have somehow mysteriously linked together! The other person ends up with only one hoop – but it is twice the size of the one he or she started out with!

What you need

Lots of old newspapers
Tape
Three pairs of scissors

Preparation

1 Cut lots of strips of newspaper, about 4 inches wide. Join them together with tape until you have three long strips, each about 3 yards long.

3 To make the second hoop, twist the paper strip *once* only before joining the ends together with tape.

2 To make the first hoop, join the two ends together with tape. Make sure that you do not get any twists in the paper.

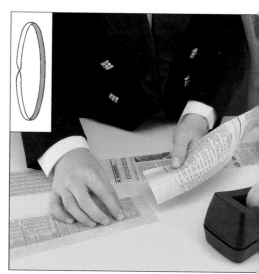

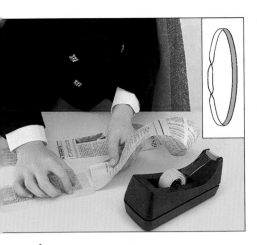

4 To make the third hoop, twist the paper strip *twice* before you join the ends together.

What you do

1 Make sure that *you* get the first hoop. (You could put a secret mark on it so that you do not make a mistake.)

2 Find two helpers. Give each of them a hoop and a pair of scissors.

3 Explain to your helpers that all three of you must cut all the way around your hoops. Tell them that it is a race to see who can do this the fastest. Tell them to be careful to stay in the middle of the strips of newspaper and not go off to one side with the scissors. Tell them to start after a count of three: "One – two – three – go!"

4 From now on the trick works on its own. It does not matter who finishes cutting first. The surprise comes when one helper ends up with two hoops magically linked together! And the other helper finds that he or she has only *one* hoop, twice as long as the original!

JAPAN: THE MAGIC SWAN

Our magic carpet now takes a short hop to another Asian country: Japan. The Japanese are known for their industry. People all over the world use Japanese computers, drive Japanese cars, and watch Japanese televisions. The Japanese also invented the amazing art of origami. This is a way of making models simply by folding pieces of paper. It is a very different type of magic. This is how you make a beautiful swan out of one piece of paper.

What you need

A square piece of paper. Use any color you'd like. Make sure it is exactly square.

What you do

1 Fold the square in half diagonally and make a crease. Open it up again.

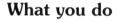

2 Fold both sides over into the center like this.

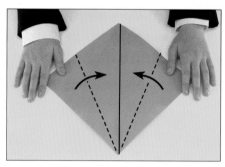

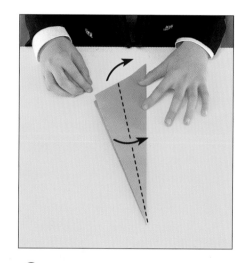

3 Fold the top half over along your original diagonal crease.

4 Now fold up both sides like this.

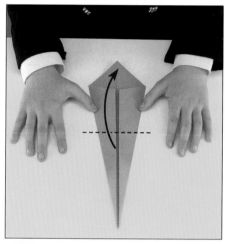

5 Open the model up, and turn it over.

6 Fold the model in half so that the two points come together.

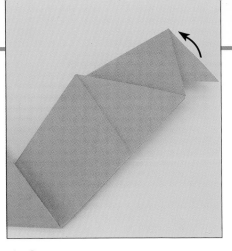

7 Fold in half down the center line by dropping both sides.

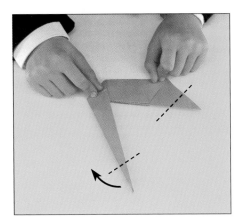

8 Pull the neck up into a more upright position and recrease the chest folds to secure it.

9 Fold down a section for the head like this. Then make two folds – back and then forward – to shape the head and beak.

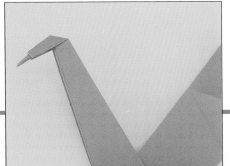

10 Fold down the back end and tuck it down inside the body. Then fold the end up again to make a sticking-up tail.

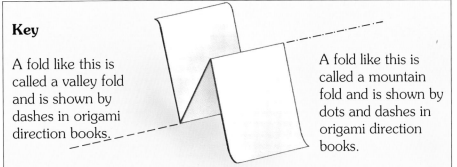

Key

A fold like this is called a valley fold and is shown by dashes in origami direction books.

A fold like this is called a mountain fold and is shown by dots and dashes in origami direction books.

FRANCE: THE MAGIC TREE

Off we go again on our magic carpet – this time to France.
In 1805, Jean-Eugène Robert-Houdin was born. When he was forty years old,
Robert-Houdin became interested in magic. And he found he was very good at it.
In fact, he was so good that he once stopped a riot by performing a magic trick!

Robert-Houdin was a great inventor of new tricks, which have been copied by many other people. He set out the basic rules of magic that all magicians now follow. As a result, he became known as the "father of modern magic." The famous Harry Houdini (see p. 14) even "stole" his name – adding an "i" on the end for good luck!

Robert-Houdin's most famous trick was to magically create a fruit tree, which then produced oranges. It was surrounded by fluttering butterflies. This is how you can make a magic tree appear.

What happens
You produce a tree, 9 feet high, from an old magazine!

What you need
An old magazine, the kind that is held together with staples. (Carefully remove the staples before you start.)
Tape
A pair of scissors

What you do

1 Take one sheet of the magazine and roll it up into a tube.

2 Take a second sheet, and place it so that it overlaps the first sheet by about 2 inches. Continue rolling so that you now have a tube made from two sheets of paper.

3 Continue in this way until you have a tube of eight sheets of paper. Keep the tube from unrolling by placing four pieces of tape along the final edge.

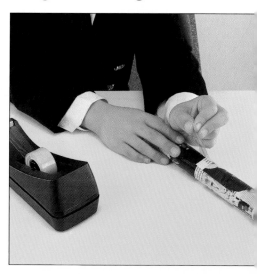

4 Stick the lower blade of the scissors into the center of the tube and make a cut down of about 4 inches. Make six cuts in this way, evenly spaced around the tube. Fold out the strips all around.

5 Stick your fingers into the center, then slowly and very carefully start to pull out the roll of paper. A tree will magically appear!

6 You should be able to make a tree at least 9 feet high!

GERMANY: THE VANISHING KEY

Now we fly across the border of France to neighboring Germany. Probably the most famous German magician was Carl Herrmann. In the nineteenth century, he put on a show using practically no props at all. (Props are all the objects and equipment used on stage in plays, shows, and movies.) He baffled the Czar (emperor) of Russia, the Sultan of Turkey, and President Abraham Lincoln. He even gave magic lessons to the Queen of Belgium. Carl was the son of a magician, Samuel Herrmann. His brother, Alexander, also became a famous magician, and was known as "Herrmann the Great." And Alexander's wife, Adelaide, was also an excellent performer. What a magical family!

Here is a trick based on the magic of Herrmann the Great.

What happens
A door key completely vanishes!

What you need
A door key with a hole or loop at the end. Ask if there is an old one at home that you can use.
A piece of elastic or rubber, 1 foot long
A safety pin
A jacket to wear
A magic wand

Preparation
Note: If you are left-handed, read *left* for *right* and *right* for *left* throughout.

1 Tie one end of the elastic to the key and the other end to the safety pin.

2 Attach the safety pin just inside the right sleeve of your jacket, at the top.

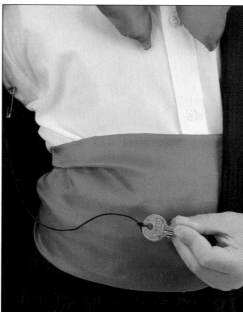

Hang the elastic down inside your sleeve. Adjust the length so that the key hangs just out of sight, about 1 inch up your sleeve.

3 Just before you perform, secretly reach into your sleeve with your left hand and pull the key down into your right hand. Grasp it firmly between your forefinger and thumb. Your hand will hide the elastic.

What you do

1 Hold the key up so that you audience can see it. Hold your left hand out, palm up.

2 Put the key into your left palm, still holding on to it with your right fingers. Close your left hand up into a fist. At the same time, let go of the key. It will shoot back up your sleeve unseen.

3 Take your right hand away and casually show that it is empty. Do not make a big thing of doing this. Keep your left hand closed.

4 Tap your left fist with your magic wand. Slowly open your hand to show that the key has completely disappeared!

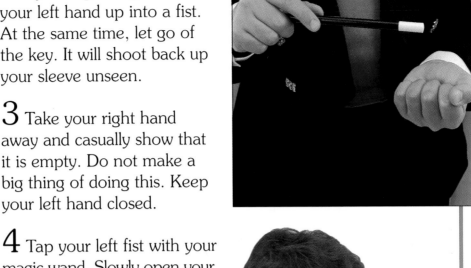

AUSTRALIA: YOU CAN'T FOOL ME!

Our magic carpet now takes us on the long journey from Europe to Australia. Australia is an enormous country. It is famous for its wild animals, such as kangaroos and duck-billed platypuses, which are not found anywhere else in the world. And you must know about boomerangs!
(What do you call a boomerang that doesn't come back? A stick!)
One famous Australian magician was Les Levante ("The Great Levante").
He died in 1978, at the age of 86, but his daughter Esme carried on his show.
Esme was an excellent magician herself.

I met The Great Levante many years ago. Here is a simple card trick he showed me.

What happens
Your friend or a member of the audience (let's call him Dean) chooses a card and puts it back in the deck. He cuts the cards over and over again. You turn your back and Dean starts turning the cards face up, calling out their names as he does so. You can tell by his voice which one is his card, no matter how hard he tries to fool you!

What you need
A deck of playing cards

What you do

1 Give Dean the deck of cards. Ask him to shuffle, then put the cards face down on the table.

2 Reach over and lift off about half the deck of cards. Ask Dean to pick up the next card, look at it, and remember it.

3 While he is doing this, slightly tilt the half of the deck that you are holding toward you, so that you can sneak a look at the bottom card. Remember this card. Let's say it is the two of hearts.

4 Tell Dean to replace his card. Put your cards back on top of the pile. The card that *you* have remembered is now on top of Dean's card.

5 Pick up all the cards and cut them. This means taking about half of the cards from the top and putting them on the bottom, in one block. Cut the cards again.

6 Now ask Dean to cut the cards as many times as he wishes. As long as they are complete cuts, and he does not drop any cards, the trick will still work. The two cards will still be together.

7 Now turn your back and ask Dean to start dealing the cards, face up on the table, calling out the name of each one as he goes. Tell him that you will be able to pick out his card, just by listening to his voice. All you have to do is listen for him to call out the two of hearts. The very next one will be *his* card.

CANADA: THE MULTIPLYING FINGERS

The final stop before home on our magic carpet ride brings us to Canada. One of today's finest magicians is the Canadian Doug Henning. You may have seen some of his television shows. He has completely changed the way magic is performed. Instead of the traditional magician's outfit of top hat, cape, and bow tie, he wears dazzling costumes using *every* color in the rainbow. He has introduced music, dancing, and story-telling into his shows.

In fact, Henning has brought us into the *modern* world of magic. Nowadays, modern science and technology have brought us incredible new inventions, which almost seem to work by magic. We have cars, airplanes, cameras, telephones, televisions, videos, space travel, computers, and solar-powered calculators.

Before we had pocket calculators, people would add numbers on their fingers. Did you know that you can multiply on your fingers? Try this.

1 Hold your hands out in front of you, with the fingers and thumbs spread out. Starting from the left, give each finger or thumb a number from one to ten.

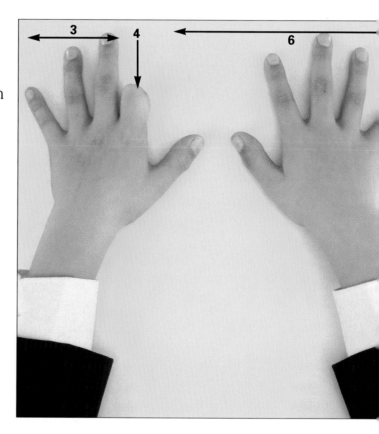

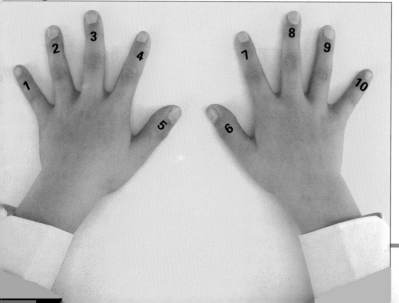

2 To multiply by nine, you only have to fold down a finger to get the answer. For example, say you want to calculate 9 x 4. Fold down finger number 4.

28

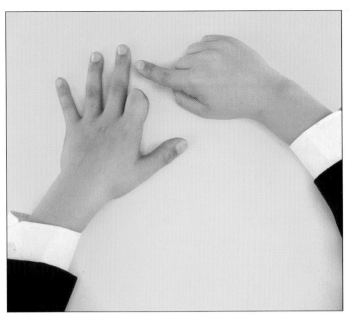

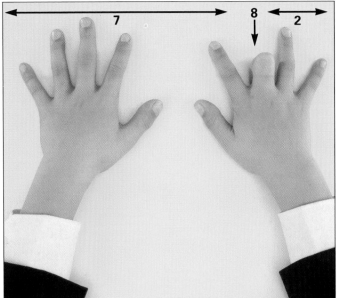

3 Look at your hands. You have three fingers to the left of your folded-down finger, and six fingers to the right: 3-6. And 9 x 4 = 36.

4 What is 9 x 8? Fold down finger number 8. There are seven fingers to the left and two fingers to the right – so the answer is 72. Simple, isn't it? The bad news is it only works when multiplying by nine.

EVERYTHING VANISHES

Finally, here is a handy trick to keep up your sleeve.
Take the trouble to learn this simple series of moves and you will be able
to make any small object "vanish." Practice with a coin.

What you do

1 Hold the coin in your left hand like this, between your thumb and forefinger.

3 Make as if to grab the coin, but as soon as it is hidden from the view of the audience by your right fingers, let the coin drop secretly into your left palm.

Remember

This trick might seem incredibly simple, but *please* practice the combination of moves until it comes completely naturally to you. Try it in front of a mirror so that you can see how it looks from the audience's point of view. You must also put on an act. If you don't seem to believe that the coin is in your right hand, your audience won't, either.

5 Now you can slowly open your right hand. The coin has vanished!

2 Bring your other hand forward to meet it. Make your right thumb go under the coin and your right fingers go over it.

4 Continue the grabbing motion with your right hand, closing it into a fist and moving it away. Do not move your left hand, just hold the hidden coin with your second and third fingers.

WHERE DO I GO FROM HERE?

I hope this book will whet your appetite and you will want to learn more about the wonderful world of magic. Here are some ideas.

Books to read

You will find many more magic books in your local library. Here is just a sample of some you might want to read.

Bailey, Vanessa. *Magic Tricks: Games and Projects.* Rainy Days. New York: Gloucester Press, 1990.

Baker, James W. *Illusions Illustrated: A Professional Magic Show for Young Performers.* Minneapolis: Lerner Publications, 1984.

Blum, Raymond. *Mathemagic.* New York: Sterling Publishing, 1992.

Day, Jon. *Let's Make Magic: Over Forty Tricks You Can Do.* New York: Kingfisher Books, 1992.

Friedhoffer, Robert. *Magic Tricks, Science Facts.* New York: Franklin Watts, 1990.

Longe, Bob. *The World's Best Coin Tricks.* New York: Sterling Publishing, 1992.

Magic clubs

Most large towns have a magic club where local magicians meet to swap ideas. It will be worth your while to join one of these clubs.

The International Brotherhood of Magicians has branches, or "rings," all over the world. For information, write to:
The International Brotherhood of Magicians Headquarters
P.O. Box 192090
St Louis, MO 63119-9998

Other organizations that might be of interest to you include:

Magical Youths International
61551 Bremen Highway
Mishawaka, IN 46544

The Society of American Magicians
P.O. Box 510260
St. Louis, MO 63151

The Association of Amateur Magicians
P.O. Box 265
Swampscott, MA 01907

Magic magazines

These will keep you up to date with the latest news and tricks. They also contain advertisements by manufacturers of magic equipment from all over the world. Write to the publishers to find out how to order copies.

Genii (monthly)
P.O. Box 36068
Los Angeles, CA 90036

Magic (monthly)
Stan Allen & Associates
7380 South Eastern Avenue
Suite 124-179
Las Vegas, NV 89123

The organizations listed above also publish newsletters and member's magazines.

American Museum of Magic

You might also want to visit the
American Museum of Magic
107 East Michigan Avenue
Marshall, MI 49068
Open daily (except Monday)

INDEX

The entries in **bold** indicate the magic tricks that are illustrated step by step.